My
First
BOOK of
Nature

Minibeasts

Victoria Munson

WAYLAND

First published in 2017 by Wayland
Copyright © Hodder and Stoughton 2017

Wayland
Carmelite House
50 Victoria Embankment
London
EC4Y 0DZ

Editor: Victoria Brooker
Designer: Elaine Wilkinson

A cataloguing record for this title is
available at the British Library.

ISBN: 978 1 5263 0151 2

Printed in China

MIX
Paper from
responsible sources
FSC
www.fsc.org
FSC® C104740

Wayland, part of Hachette Children's Group
and published by Hodder
and Stoughton Limited.
www.hachette.co.uk

Acknowledgements:
Alamy/The Wildlife Studio 10; iStockphoto.com 11
eli_asenova; Shutterstock.com: cover centre Vitalili
Hulai; tr (stag beetle) alslutsky; t (honey bees) Peter
Waters; bl (swallowtail butterfly caterpillar) Anest; br
(snail) EsHanPhot; (ladybirds) irin-k; 2, rpt 16 Marek
Velechovsky; 3b, rpt 13 goran cakmazovic; 3t Arto
Hakola; 3b Zdenek Kubik; 4 mikeledray; 5 Suede
Chen; 7t Bruce MacQueen; 7b Karel Gallas; 8 Pavel
Krasensky; 9t Sue Robinson; 9b Stephan Morris;
10b StevenRussellSmithPhotos; 10t Bachkova
Natalia; 11t Ger Bosma Photos; 11b Henrik Larsson;
12r colin Robert varndell; 12l Kuttelvaserova
Stuchelova; 13t goran cakmazovic; 13b Greg Gillies;
15t ChiccoDodiFC; 14 Hermit crab; 15b IanRedding;
16b Marek Velechovsky; 16t Chris Moody; 17
IanRedding; 18b Ezume Images; 18t Steve Byland;
19t Philippova Anastasia; 19 Arno van Dulmen;
20 kingfisher; 20t David Peter Ryan; 21 Maryna
Pleshkun; 22r Vectomart; 22l benchart;
23 NotionPic

Contents

What is a minibeast?   4

Beetles   6

Pond Minibeasts   8

Butterflies   10

Wasps and Bees   12

Seaside Minibeasts   14

Millipedes, Centipedes
   and Woodlice   16

Slugs, Snails and Spiders   18

Ants, Worms and Earwigs   20

Where to find Minibeasts   22

Glossary and Index   24

What is a Minibeast?

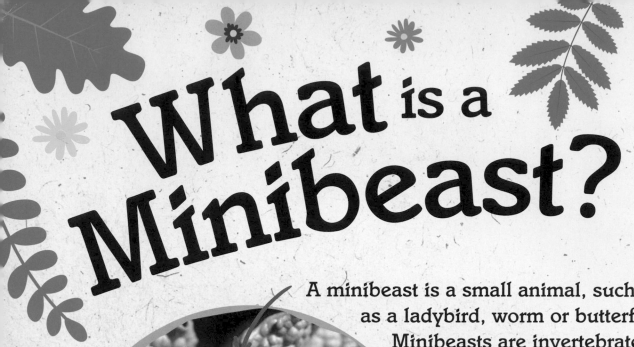

A minibeast is a small animal, such as a ladybird, worm or butterfly. Minibeasts are invertebrates, which means animals without a backbone.

Minibeasts do not have a skeleton in their bodies, so their bodies are soft and bendy.

To protect their bodies some minibeasts, such as snails, have a hard shell.

Many minibeasts use antennae, hairs or even feet to taste, smell and touch. Snails use antennae to smell with.

Butterflies use their feet to taste with.

Minibeasts can be found in many different types of habitat, from gardens and woodlands to ponds and lakes.

Minibeasts are also called bugs or creepy crawlies.

Beetles

Ladybirds are a type of beetle. Many ladybirds have red wings with black spots. The bright red colour warns predators that it will taste horrible.

Some ladybirds are yellow, orange or black. Some ladybirds have stripes or patches.

Ladybirds can beat their wings 85 times a second.

Soldier beetles are orangey-red. Their bright colour is a warning to predators to stay away.

In summer, look for soldier beetles on cow parsley flowerheads.

Stag beetles are Britain's largest beetle.

Stag beetles get their name from their large jaws, which look like a stag deer's antlers.

Stag beetles use their jaws to fight other stag beetles.

Pond Minibeasts

Backswimmers swim upside-down. While moving, their legs look like the oars on a rowing boat.

They are also known as water boatman.

Backswimmers are carnivores, which means they eat other animals, such as insects, fish and tadpoles.

Pond skaters are small bugs that can walk on water.

They have tiny hairs on their feet that repel water and allow them to 'skate' on the surface.

Dragonflies can be many different colours from red, brown and orange to bright green or blue.

Look for dragonflies hovering over the top of ponds looking for food.

Dragonflies have large eyes to help them detect prey.

Butterflies

Peacock butterflies get their name from the yellow and blue eyespots on their wings.

These spots look like the markings on a peacock bird.

In winter, peacock butterflies hibernate in hollow trees and sheds.

Red Admiral butterflies have black and red patterns on their wings.

Red Admirals like to suck juices from rotting fruit.

Large white and small white butterflies look similar, but one is much bigger than the other.

Large and small white butterflies are also known as cabbage whites because the caterpillars love to eat cabbages and sprouts.

Caterpillars are long and worm-like, with six legs. In spring and summer, caterpillars will turn into butterflies.

Wasps and Bees

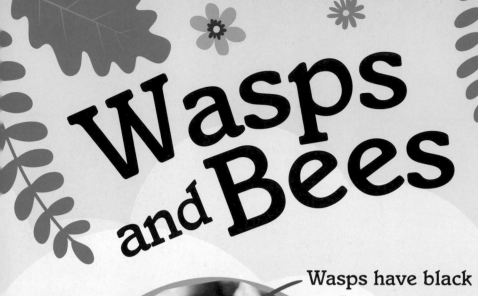

Wasps have black and yellow stripes. Large groups of wasps live together in nests.

There can be up to 2,000 wasps in one nest.

The nests are usually in holes in the ground.

You can tell hornets from wasps because hornets have brown and yellow stripes, not black and yellow. Hornets are also twice as big.

Honey bees have brown-black bodies with orangey-yellow bands.

Honey bees sting when they feel threatened, but once they have stung they die, unlike wasps, which can sting again and again.

The most common bumblebee in Britain is the buff-tailed bumblebee.

Buff-tailed bumblebees have black and yellow stripes with a white tail.

Seashore Minibeasts

Hermit crabs don't have their own shell. They live inside the empty shell of other animals, such as periwinkles and whelks.

A crab's soft body is protected in a shell.

Hard, red pincers stick out of the shell, helping them to move and catch food.

Mussels have oval, bluish-purplish shells. Mussel shells are tightly closed out of the water, but underwater they open to take in food.

With their tentacles hidden away, beadlet anemones look like jelly-shaped blobs attached to rocks.

Beadlet anemones can be red, green or brown. They use their tentacles to sting prey and drag it into their body to eat.

One beadlet anemone can have up to 192 tentacles.

15

Centipedes, Millipedes and Woodlice

Centipedes are reddish-brown. They are carnivores and will even eat other centipedes.

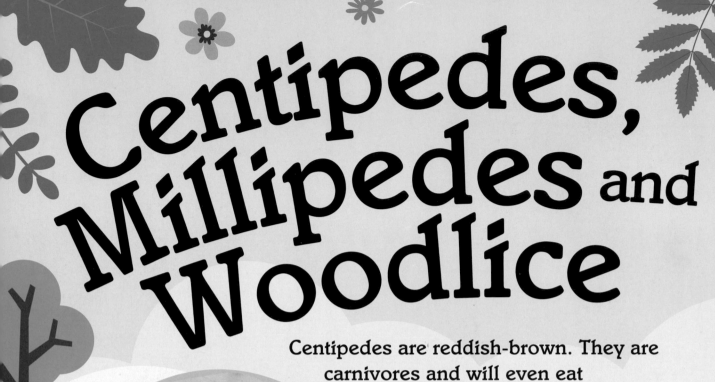

Some centipedes do have over 100 legs, but the most common UK centipede has just 30 legs.

Centipedes live in the soil, hidden beneath rocks, logs or tree bark.

Millipedes have between 40 and 400 legs. Some millipedes give out a smelly liquid to put off predators.

When millipedes are frightened, they roll up into a ball.

This millipede is called a white-legged snake millipede.

Woodlice have a hard outer shell called an exoskeleton.

Woodlice have 14 legs and two antennae. Look for woodlice under rocks or logs.

Woodlice are eaten by centipedes, spiders and toads.

Slugs, Snails and Spiders

Garden slugs are grey-black and grow to about 4 cm long.

Slugs have two pairs of tentacles. One pair is used for seeing and smelling. The other pair is for feeling and tasting.

Slugs prefer wet and damp weather because they will dry out in very hot weather.

Snails live in dark, damp and moist places, such as in undergrowth and near soil.

As snails get older, their shells get thicker.

Garden spiders have eight legs and a hard outer skeleton. They are carnivores, which means they eat meat.

Spiders spin webs to catch their prey.

Garden spiders are grey-brown or reddish brown and have a large white cross on their backs.

Ants, Earwigs and Worms

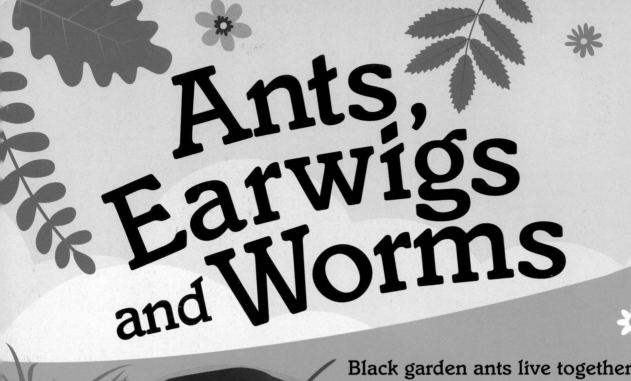

Black garden ants live together in huge nests on the ground.

A black ant nest can contain more than 5,000 ants.

Ant nests can be found in paving stones, in between bricks or in soil.

Ants come into houses to look for sweet foods, such as jam or sugar.

Earwigs have pincers at the end of their body. Earwigs are mostly nocturnal, coming out to feed at night.

In the daytime, look under flower pots, logs and stones to find them.

Earwigs got their name because of their ear-shaped wings, although they rarely fly.

Earthworms live in the soil. Their soft bodies are made up of segments. They have a mouth, but they don't have eyes or a nose.

Use a magnifying glass to look at the hairs on a worm's skin.

Earthworms have many predators, including birds, hedgehogs and foxes.

Where to find Minibeasts

Many minibeasts hibernate, or spend the winter as eggs, so the best time to look for them is in late spring or summer. Look for minibeasts in these habitats.

1

Under a log
Woodlice, earwigs

2

In the soil
Worms, ants, centipedes, millipedes

3

In gardens and parks
Caterpillars, butterflies, bumblebees, honey bees, beetles

4

In undergrowth
Snails, slugs

5

Around ponds
Backswimmers, pond skaters, dragonflies

How many minibeasts can you find? If you move any minibeasts from their habitat, always put them back where you found them.

Glossary and Index

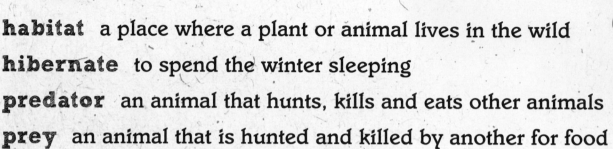

habitat a place where a plant or animal lives in the wild

hibernate to spend the winter sleeping

predator an animal that hunts, kills and eats other animals

prey an animal that is hunted and killed by another for food

ant 20
backswimmer 8
beadlet anemone 15
bumblebee 13
butterfly 5, 10-11
  large white 11
  peacock 10
  red admiral 10
  small white 11
caterpillar 11
centipede 16

dragonfly 9
earwig 5, 21
earthworm 21
habitat 5, 22-23
hermit crab 14
honey bee 13
hornet 12
invertebrate 4
ladybird 4, 5
millipede 17
mussel 15

pond skater 9
slug 5, 18
snail 4, 19
spider 19
soldier beetle 7
stag beetle 7
water boatman 8
wasp 12
woodlice 17

Birds
9781526301208

What is a Bird?
Garden Birds
City Birds
Woodland Birds
Ducks, Swans and Geese
Birds of Prey
Owls
Farmland Birds
Follow that Footprint
Glossary and Index

Flowers
9781526301499

What are flowers?
Garden flowers
Park flowers
Seashore flowers
Mountain flowers
Water flowers
Meadow flowers
Heathland flowers
Woodland flowers
Flower life cycle
Glossary and index

Mammals
9781526301475

What is a Mammal?
Hedgehogs and Moles
Badgers and Foxes
Rabbits and Hares
Mice and Rats
Squirrels
Voles and Shrews
Stoats and Weasels
Deer
Follow that Footprint
Glossary and Index

Minibeasts
9781526301512

What are minibeasts?
Beetles
Bugs
Butterflies
Wasps and Bees
Seaside minibeasts
Millipedes, Centipedes
    and Woodlice
Slugs, snails and spiders
Ants, worms and earwigs
Where to find minibeasts
Glossary and index

Seashore
9781526301536

What is the seashore?
Rock pool creatures
Seaweed
Shells
Birds
Insects
Fish
Mammals
Plants
Seashore shells
Glossary and index

Trees
9781526301550

What is a tree?
Oaks
Willows
Silver birch, Alder, Hazel
Sycamore, Field Maple,
    London Plane
Lime, Rowan, Whitebeam
Chestnuts and Beech
Yew, Monkey Puzzle, Juniper
Scots Pine, Norway Spruce,
    Douglas Fir
Leaves and seeds
Glossary and index